A. Owers

FOLENS

IDEAS BANK GRAMMAR

Chris Webster

Contents

Folens Publishers

How to use this book

Ideas Bank books provide ready to use, practical, photocopiable activity pages for children, **plus** a wealth of ideas for extension and development.

TEACHER IDEAS PAGE

PHOTOCOPIABLE ACTIVITY PAGE

Background information and other help given.

Suggestions for developing work on the photocopiable pages.

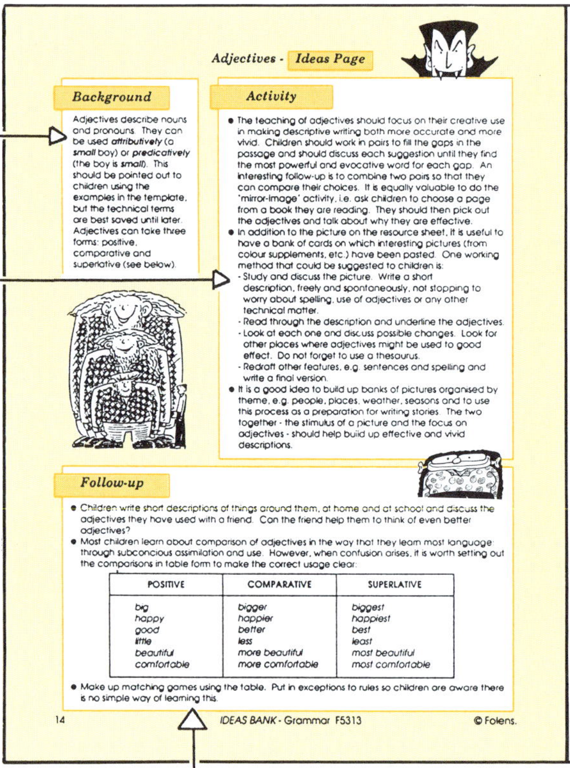

Adjectives - *Ideas Page*

Background

Adjectives describe nouns and pronouns. They can be used ***attributively*** (a ***small*** boy) or ***predicatively*** (the boy is ***small***). This should be pointed out to children using the examples in the template, but the technical terms are best saved until later. Adjectives can take three forms: positive, comparative and superlative (see below).

Activity

- The teaching of adjectives should focus on their creative use in making descriptive writing both more accurate and more vivid. Children should work in pairs to fill the gaps in the passage and should discuss each suggestion until they find the most powerful and evocative word for each gap. An interesting follow-up is to combine two pairs so that they can compare their choices. It is equally valuable to do the 'mirror-image' activity, i.e. ask children to choose a page from a book they are reading. They should then pick out the adjectives and talk about why they are effective.
- In addition to the picture on the resource sheet, it is useful to have a bank of cards on which interesting pictures (from colour supplements, etc.) have been pasted. One working method that could be suggested to children is:
  - Study and discuss the picture. Write a short description, freely and spontaneously, not stopping to worry about spelling, use of adjectives or any other technical matter.
  - Read through the description and underline the adjectives.
  - Look at each one and discuss possible changes. Look for other places where adjectives might be used to good effect. Do not forget to use a thesaurus.
  - Redraft other features, e.g. sentences and spelling and write a final version.
- It is a good idea to build up banks of pictures organised by theme, e.g. people, places, weather, seasons and to use this process as a preparation for writing stories. The two together - the stimulus of a picture and the focus on adjectives - should help buiid up effective and vivid descriptions.

Follow-up

- Children write short descriptions of things around them, at home and at school and discuss the adjectives they have used with a friend. Can the friend help them to think of even better adjectives?
- Most children learn about comparison of adjectives in the way that they learn most language: through subconcious assimilation and use. However, when confusion arises, it is worth setting out the comparisons in table form to make the correct usage clear:

POSITIVE	COMPARATIVE	SUPERLATIVE
big	*bigger*	*biggest*
happy	*happier*	*happiest*
good	*better*	*best*
little	*less*	*least*
beautiful	*more beautiful*	*most beautiful*
comfortable	*more comfortable*	*most comfortable*

- Make up matching games using the table. Put in exceptions to rules so children are aware there is no simple way of learning this.

14 *IDEAS BANK* - Grammar F5313 © Folens.

Adjectives

Adjectives

An adjective is a describing word. It gives more information about a noun, e.g.

The ghost gave a heavy sigh.
The little girl hid under the bedclothes.
The house was haunted.

Work in pairs to fill the gaps with suitable adjectives.

Varney the Vampire climbed in through the ________ window. He saw a ________ four-poster bed where a ________ girl was sleeping. He bared his ________ teeth in a ________ snarl and crept towards her. He paused to admire her beauty. She had ________ hair, her ________ eyes were ________, her lips were ________ but above all her neck was ________. Varney leaned over and sank his fangs into her ________ skin. She let out a ________ scream, but it was too late.

NOW

Work in pairs to describe this picture. Use adjectives to make your description as vivid as possible.

© Folens. *IDEAS BANK* - Grammar F5313 15

Extension activities suggested to take the work one step further.

Independent activities for children to work with.

- Time-saving, relevant and practical, **Ideas Bank** books ensure that you will always have work readily to hand.

Cover by: In Touch Creative Services Ltd. Illustrations by: Eric Jones. Cover Photo: Gary S. Chapman (The Image Bank).

First published 1993 by Folens Limited, Albert House, Apex Business Centre, Boscombe Road, Dunstable, LU5 4RL, England.

ISBN 185276531-3 Printed in Singapore by Craft Print

Introduction

This book, and its companion, Ideas Bank *Punctuation*, provide a programme for the teaching of basic secretarial language skills to children aged 7-11 years. There is much more to language than the basic skills covered in these two books so the activities need to be combined with broader aspects of language work and, above all, with critical reading and creative writing.

Before describing how the system works, it is important to establish some parameters.

- *Native speakers of a language have internalised most of its grammatical rules. However, they will need help where local dialect varies from standard English and where written forms differ from spoken forms.*
- *Children need some simple terminology so that they can discuss their language work with other children and the teacher.*
- *They need to be taught the numerous conventions of written English such as the use of capital letters, punctuation and paragraphing.*
- *They need to be taught a more conscious control over the stylistic features of written English; for example, how to increase the descriptive power of sentences and how to combine statements in different ways to achieve exactly the effect they want.*
- *We must also bear in mind the paradox that those children who most need help are least likely to understand grammatical concepts and abstract explanations. This means that much of our grammar teaching must be rule of thumb, practical and in the context of the children's own writing.*

Pages containing key teaching points have a **template** at the top of the resource sheet. These templates provide a brief explanation of the grammatical point plus an example. They can be cut out and pasted into children's notebooks as reminders, made into wall charts, made into a pack of reference cards, or perhaps stapled together and made into a booklet.

The photocopiable sheets can be used in a variety of ways (see page 48). They should be stored in an easily accessible place and can then be used as follows:

Each child is paired with a writing partner who can be consulted at any stage during writing. Each has a redrafting checklist (see page 47) which is used for self-review and as a basis for discussions with the writing partner and the teacher.

The child writes the first draft. His/her writing partner is consulted using the drafting checklist. The teacher is consulted if necessary.

The construction of sentences (for example) is identified for redrafting. The child, writing partner or teacher selects the appropriate worksheet.

Advice and support on the other areas of the drafting checklist may be needed, e.g. appropriateness to intended audience.

The child reads the explanation on the worksheet and tries to correct his/her work. Practice exercises can be used if necessary. Work can be checked with the writing partner or teacher.

The child incorporates what he/she has learned from all aspects of the redrafting process - checklists, discussions, etc. in the final draft.

The materials in this book are intended to be used with the whole junior age range, beginning with simple work on parts of speech and moving on to more sophisticated work on sentence building.

Background

- The parts of speech are simply a way of classifying words according to the way they are used grammatically. Modern linguists have suggested alternatives, and more precise forms of classification, but the traditional parts of speech are still used in most language teaching.
- It is important to realise that there is little merit in being able to say the parts of speech by rote. The value of learning them is that knowledge of how they work helps children to write better. Nouns, adjectives, pronouns, verbs and adverbs are covered in detail and conjunctions are covered in the 'Sentences' section.
- The three remaining parts of speech are less important. Most pupils will use the correct prepositions automatically through long association, though a few continue to give problems, e.g. different than/different from/different to? These can be dealt with as they arise. Interjections will also be used naturally by children, though there is an interesting teaching point in that they need exclamation marks. Grammarians differ as to whether articles should be included under parts of speech, but they are included here for the sake of completeness.
- There are two main teaching points about articles. The obvious one is to make sure children understand the rule for using 'an' instead of 'a' (when the word following begins with a vowel). A more interesting point is when there is a stylistic choice between the definite article (the) and the indefinite article (a/an).

For example, children could discuss the difference between sentences like:

- *he ate an apple* — *he ate the apple*
- *a girl ran into the room* — *the girl ran into the room*
- *it was a diamond* — *it was the diamond*

Follow-up

Learning parts of speech is not easy because they are abstract concepts. Do not expect too much at once. Try the following strategies:

- When talking about books and writing, try to name the parts of speech, e.g. instead of saying "Can you think of a more exciting 'word' here?" say "Can you think of a more exciting 'adjective' here?"
- Introduce them one at a time. The following order is recommended:
  - noun and adjective
  - verb and adverb (these words create the basic structure of language and build its descriptive power)
  - pronoun and conjunction (these terms can be introduced when children need help in constructing more sophisticated sentences)
  - prepositions (the study of these is mainly a matter of correct usage)
  - interjections, articles.

Activities

The poem is useful to give children an overview and as a mnemonic aid.

- Children can be asked to learn it in pairs and test each other. It can then be recalled whenever any discussion about words takes place.
- Children find their own examples and rewrite some of the key verses. An alternative approach would be to make these into four or six line verses.
- Blank out the names of the parts of speech and ask children to fill in the blanks using the definitions and examples as clues.
- Ask children to rewrite the poem in simple prose, but with many more examples of the main parts of speech.
- Working in groups, children could prepare a 'performance' of the poem to music using percussion instruments and electronic keyboards. Not only is this fun, but it is a powerful aid to the memory. It also helps to reinforce the concept of rhythm.

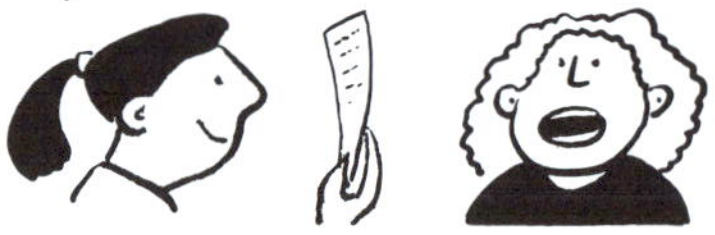

Parts of Speech

The easiest way to learn the parts of speech is to learn this poem.

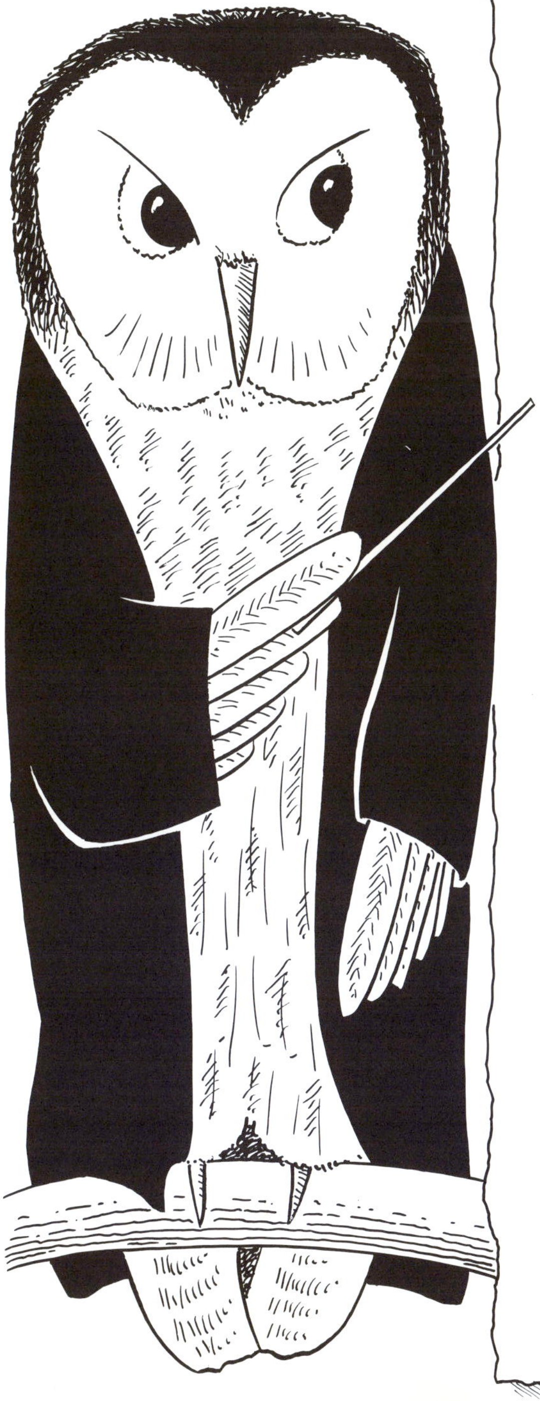

A noun's the name of any thing
As ***school****, or* ***garden****,* ***hoop*** *or* ***swing****.*

Adjectives describe the noun
As ***great****,* ***small****,* ***pretty****,* ***white*** *or* ***brown****.*

Instead of nouns the pronouns stand -
Her *head,* ***his*** *face,* ***your*** *arm,* ***my*** *hand.*

Verbs tell of something being done -
To ***read****,* ***write****,* ***count****,* ***sing****,* ***jump*** *or* ***run****.*

How, when and where the adverbs tell,
As ***slowly****,* ***near****,* ***now*** *or* ***well****.*

Conjunctions join the words together,
As men ***and*** *women, wind* ***or*** *weather.*

The preposition stands before
A noun, as ***in*** *or* ***through*** *a door.*

The interjection shows surprise,
As ***Oh****, how pretty!* ***Ah****, how wise!*

Three little words you often see,
Are articles - ***a****,* ***an*** *and* ***the****.*

The whole are called Nine Parts of Speech,
Which reading, writing, speaking teach.

NOW ● Add other examples to each list.

Nouns - Ideas Page

Background

- A noun is the name of a person, place or thing. It is often introduced by a determiner such as a, the, or some. Its ending can change to express singular, plural or possessive.

Activities

- The **Nouns** activity sheet introduces children to the symbolic representation of nouns by the Ancient Egyptians.
- Children could explore hieroglyphs further and may be particularly interested in the so-called Hieroglyphic Alphabet. This was a series of signs used to represent sounds so that foreign names could be spelled. A simplified version is given below.
  Children could be asked to discuss which noun-picture each sign developed from.

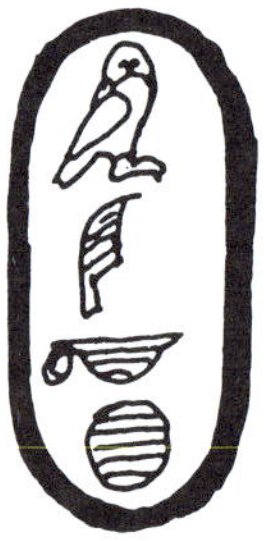

Follow-up

- Most modern appliances are sold worldwide so symbols are used instead of words. The symbols are explained in the handbook which will have sections in many different languages. Ask children to draw one of the following and label the controls with symbols:
  - a microwave oven
  - a car dashboard
  - a camera
  - a radio-cassette recorder
  - a video-recorder
  - a washing machine.

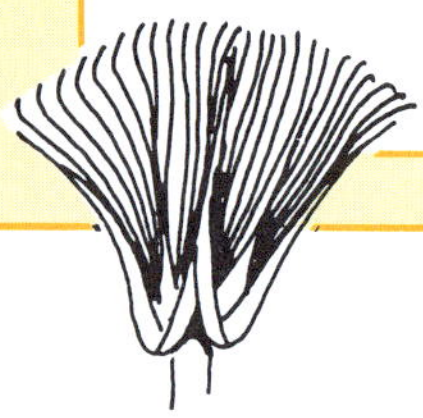

- Ask them to find as many symbols as they can to make a wall display. Road signs are another form of sign language that are used all around the world. Ask children to draw as many road signs as they can and label them.
- A useful follow-up to these activities is to ask children to write a story using picture symbols for nouns only, then to give them to their partners to read. This should help to make the nature of common nouns clearer. There are many nouns, such as abstract nouns, which are difficult to draw.
- If children are having difficulty identifying nouns, ask the following questions: 'Can you pick it up?' That will cover literally thousands of nouns. Larger items can be included simply and humorously by saying, 'Could you pick it up if you had super powers?' Leave abstract nouns until later!
- It is important to encourage children to identify nouns in their own work, whether in reading or writing. For example, they could find the noun which is the subject of the sentence, develop the noun phrase, or discuss how writers have done this.

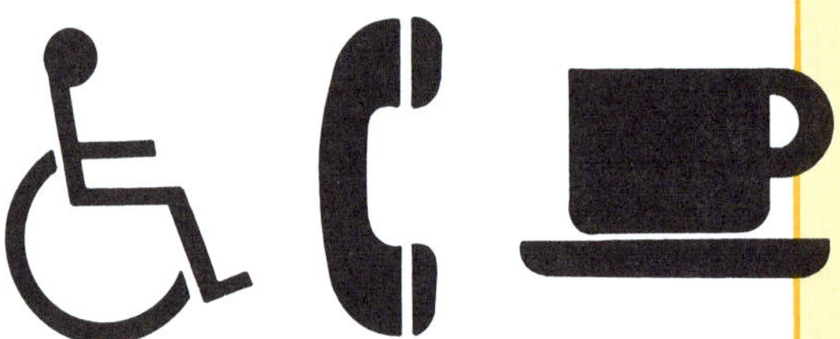

Nouns

Nouns

A noun is a naming word. Nouns are used to name people, places or things.

People	Places	Things
girl woman doctor	park city fun fair	wasp pen book

Add your own examples to the list.

We can draw most nouns. Many early writing systems are based on this idea. Guess what nouns these Egyptian hieroglyphs stand for.

m	f	p	b
	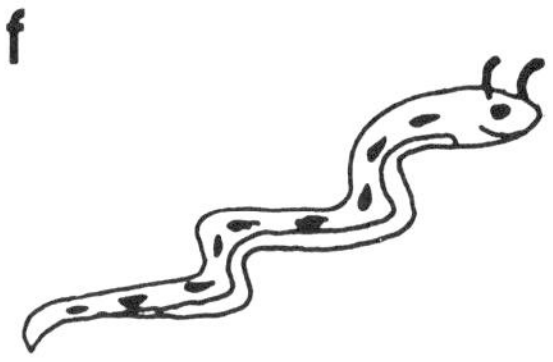	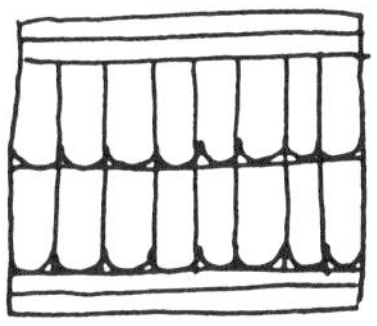	

- Invent hieroglyphs for runner, happiness, many, wisdom, truth, surprise. Which of these words are nouns?

NOW Complete this story in which all the nouns have been drawn as pictures.

 got on the 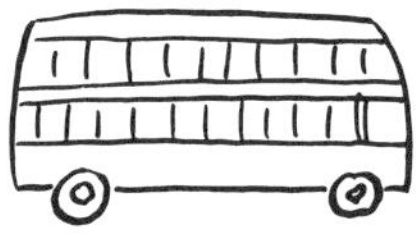 to go to . She sat on her  and read her .

Proper Nouns - Ideas Page

Background

- There are several types of noun - proper, common, concrete and abstract.
- It would be unnecessarily confusing to teach them all. However, there is particular value in teaching proper nouns.
- Proper nouns are specific names, e.g. people, places, brand names, days, months and special occasions. For this reason, proper nouns begin with a capital letter. Thus teaching proper nouns helps children to use capital letters more effectively as well as increasing their knowledge about nouns.
  Note:
  - proper nouns do not usually have plurals but there are exceptions, e.g. The Robinsons are coming for dinner.
  - they are not usually used with determiners (e.g. a, the, some).

Activities

- This sorting exercise is designed to help children work out for themselves some of the properties of proper nouns, particularly that they are the names of specific items and that they all begin with capital letters.
- When the activity is finished it is important to sum up to consolidate what children have learned. The simple definition given could be discussed and then followed up by the wall display described below.

Follow-up

- Logos are part of the 'razzmatazz' of the media world that young people find fascinating. Choose several exciting logos to show to your children and ask them to make up their own. This is most effective if linked in a cross-curricular way to a technology project. They can think up a company name and a product name and design the logo for it.
- Creating a display is a valuable way of reinforcing the uniqueness of proper nouns. Ask children to find examples of brand names (bring in articles where possible, e.g. sweet wrappings), names of buildings (ask them to sketch the sign so that its size and style can be discussed, e.g. 'The Red Lion'), magazines, newspapers and books. Not only will many of the proper nouns collected begin with a capital letter, but they will be designed to stand out. The techniques used will form an interesting discussion point.
  Look for:
  - colour
  - type styles
  - logos
  - size
  - positioning.
- Children can respond by using some of the design features for their own names, book covers, etc.
- Look for brand names in magazine advertisements, cereal packets and sweet wrappings. Make lists of names of the people in the class. Make full size street signs for some of the streets in the local area (try to copy the shape and type of writing). Make a list of local shops. Make copies of their signs, trying to use the same style of writing, colours and shapes.
- **Name strings**
  This game helps to reinforce the idea of names as proper nouns and the need for capital letters to begin proper nouns. Children decide whether they are playing 'people' or 'places'. Child one writes down a name. Child two must think of another name beginning with the last letter of the first name. For every correct turn, a child wins a point. If a child forgets to use a capital letter a point is lost.

Proper Nouns

Proper Nouns

A proper noun is the name of a person, place, brand name, day, month and special occasion.

Person	Place	Brand Name	Day/Month/ Special Occasion
James Mr Roberts Elvis Presley	California Wales Elm Avenue	Coke Nintendo Rover	Monday August Hallowe'en

Add your own examples to the list.

Below are some nouns.

- Circle the proper nouns.

street *ghost* *Germany*

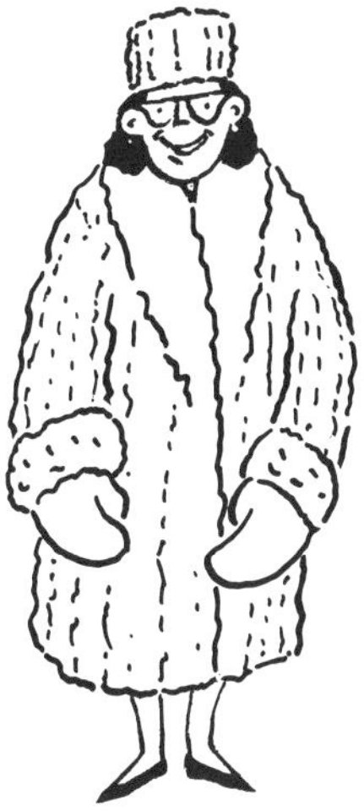

typewriter *Ms Mitten* *Southampton*

Roberta *Fido* *chair* *planet*

Mars *Mr Crystal*

North Street *pencil* *bush* *coach*

- What do you notice about the first letter of all the proper nouns?

Background

Most nouns have a singular and plural form. The majority simply add -s. However there are a small number of irregular forms.

Activities

- The first teaching point is to ensure that children understand what the terms singular and plural mean. This can be reinforced by asking them to add their own examples to the template grid on the activity sheet.
- The majority of plurals will cause no difficulty, but there are a few which are the cause of many spelling mistakes. The two commonest, irregular plurals and -ys/-ies plurals, are explored on the activity sheet. When children are confident with these, they can then explore -fs/-ves plurals. Note that some plurals can now be spelled either way, e.g. hoofs/hooves and that there is a move towards the more standard -fs endings.

FS/VES PLURALS

half	halves
leaf	leaves
thief	thieves
wolf	wolves
self	selves
knife	knives

The following points should be dealt with as they arise:

- Some -oes endings may been seen in print, e.g. cargoes, but in most cases it is also correct to spell them without the ***e***, e.g. cargos. Keep to the latter and avoid confusion.
- Numbers and abbreviations take an apostrophe before the plural, e.g. 'in the 1970s'.
- Compound plurals, e.g. 'mothers-in-law' behave in several different ways, and should be dealt with individually.
- **Play plural maths.** One donkey plus one donkey equals? Seven babies divided by seven equals? This can provide a quick, fun spelling test.

Follow-up

- Play the plurals game. Write singular words on cards and take it in turns to pick one out and write the plural. This could be prepared in advance as follows:
  - To avoid the problem of children constantly asking whether a plural is correct, the words can be written on folded slips of paper, with the correct plural written inside the fold. The folded papers are placed in a box and mixed up before playing.
  - A quick way of providing a list of words is to use the resource sheet on page 13.
- **Another plural game.** Children play in pairs. Each child should write a short story (three or four lines is long enough - abler and older pupils could write more) in the singular, e.g.

  I went into a haunted house. It was very quiet. Then a mouse squeaked. I thought it was a ghost and I ran away.

- Children swap their stories and read them to each other in the plural. There will be lots of fun as all sorts of unexpected pitfalls are found. Children will also learn more about plurals, e.g. making pronouns plural.
- Continue to teach the correct use of plurals on a day-to-day basis by:
  - making large posters to remind children of irregular, -y/-ies, and -fs/-ves plurals
  - not treating problems with plurals as spelling mistakes - use a different correction code, e.g. *PL*

Singular and Plural

Singular and Plural

Most nouns can be singular or plural. Singular means one, plural means more than one.

Singular	Plural
tree	trees
house	houses

Add your own examples to the list.

Most plurals are formed by adding -s, e.g. tree, trees, but others add other letters.

- Write the plural of these words.

child ____________ sheep ____________
mouse ____________ woman ____________
foot ____________ goose ____________
tooth ____________ ox ____________
person

-y/-ies Plurals

NOW

Confusion between -y and -ies is the cause of many spelling mistakes! This is the rule: words ending in -y change to -ies if the letter before -y is a consonant.

- Write out the correct plural for these words.

dictionary ____________ donkey ____________
balcony ____________ ceremony ____________
fly ____________ baby ____________
chimney ____________ story ____________
industry ____________ lorry ____________

Write a funny story using some of these plurals

Noun on Noun - Ideas Page

Background

- Nouns are often put together to form new words or concepts. Sometimes the words are joined, as in 'newspaper', and sometimes not, as in 'newspaper boy'.

Activity

- The noun on noun game allows children to explore noun combinations in a creative way.
- The nouns are cut out, shuffled and placed face-down in the centre of the table. Children take turns to select any two cards. They turn the cards over and use them either way round to make a new word or concept.
- For example, if a child turned over the words 'street' and 'bed' they could be arranged as 'street bed' or 'bed street'. He/she then has to use his/her imagination to describe the new thing, e.g.

  'A street bed is a special bed for sleeping in the street. It has a roof, a door and a window. It has four wheels so that it can be moved around easily.'

  If it sounds even remotely plausible, a point has been won.
- Sometimes it will be easy, e.g. 'school' and 'girl'; sometimes difficult, e.g. 'school' and 'baby' (baby school), 'river' and 'lake'. In cases like the latter the player may well ask to 'pass'.
- The winner is the one who scores most points, but really all are winners because the game is great fun and it increases knowledge about language.

Follow-up

- Some of the combinations generated by the game may well sow the seed for a longer piece of writing. For example, the 'Baby School' mentioned above could be a school for ambitious parents who want their babies to grow up to be geniuses. Babies as young as six months are taught long division and how to play the violin. They learn to read using Shakespeare instead of reading schemes. Children could write a prospectus for such a school or the story of over-ambitious parents who made their child very unhappy by sending them to such a school. The possibilities are endless!
- To extend this activity children could work in groups of four or five to brainstorm a set of 'adjective cards'. These can be added to the game to make it even more fun.
- The noun on noun cards could also be used to generate nonsense poems. Children shuffle the cards in separate packs and deal them as follows:

  adjective noun adjective noun
  noun noun
  adjective adjective noun
  noun

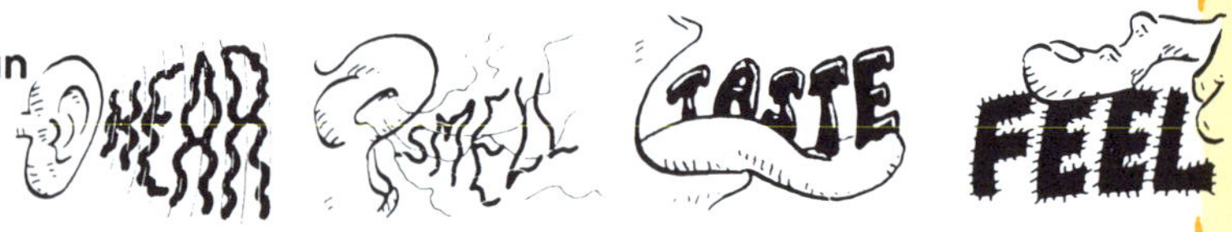

- They could also make up their own combinations.
- When they have finished playing the game, give some time for a 'free writing' session in which they are asked to develop any good combinations of words that have been created.
- Lantern poems are written in the shape of a Japanese lantern. Work with five lines:
  - a noun (one syllable)
  - word(s) to describe the noun (three syllables)
  - word(s) to describe the noun (four syllables)
  - a noun (one syllable)
- Cut out large shapes, colour them, write the poems inside and display by hanging from the ceiling.

Noun on Noun

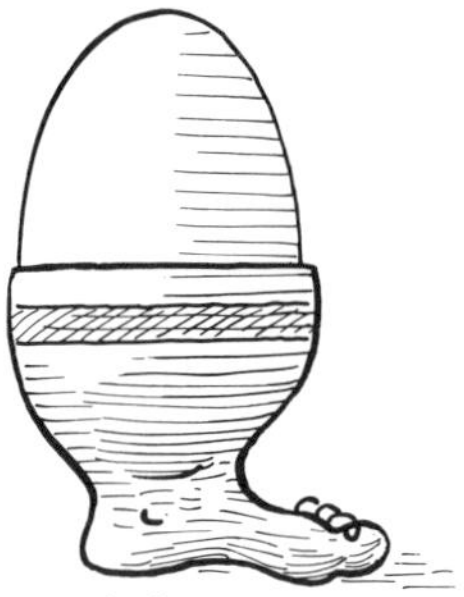

Cut out the nouns, shuffle them and take it in turns to pick out two nouns to create a new idea. Use your imagination to describe the idea.
e.g. What could an 'address factory' be?

actor	address	animal	artist	baby	ball
bank	battle	beach	bed	bird	book
bottle	box	boy	bridge	bus	camp
car	castle	cat	chair	child	city
class	coat	computer	country	crowd	daughter
day	desk	doctor	dream	dress	driver
ear	egg	eye	face	factory	farm
field	finger	foot	friend	game	garden
girl	hall	hand	handle	hat	head
heart	horse	hospital	hotel	house	island

Adjectives - Ideas Page

Background

Adjectives describe nouns and pronouns. They can be used ***attributively*** (a ***small*** boy) or ***predicatively*** (the boy is ***small***). This should be pointed out to children using the examples in the template, but the technical terms are best saved until later. Adjectives can take three forms: positive, comparative and superlative (see below).

Activity

- The teaching of adjectives should focus on their creative use in making descriptive writing both more accurate and more vivid. Children should work in pairs to fill the gaps in the passage and should discuss each suggestion until they find the most powerful and evocative word for each gap. An interesting follow-up is to combine two pairs so that they can compare their choices. It is equally valuable to do the 'mirror-image' activity, i.e. ask children to choose a page from a book they are reading. They should then pick out the adjectives and talk about why they are effective.
- In addition to the picture on the activity sheet, it is useful to have a bank of cards on which interesting pictures (from colour supplements, etc.) have been pasted. One working method that could be suggested to children is:
  - Study and discuss the picture. Write a short description, freely and spontaneously, not stopping to worry about spelling, use of adjectives or any other technical matter.
  - Read through the description and underline the adjectives.
  - Look at each one and discuss possible changes. Look for other places where adjectives might be used to good effect. Do not forget to use a thesaurus.
  - Redraft other features, e.g. sentences and spelling, and write a final version.
- It is a good idea to build up banks of pictures organised by theme, e.g. people, places, weather, seasons and to use this process as a preparation for writing stories. The two together - the stimulus of a picture and the focus on adjectives - should help build up effective and vivid descriptions.

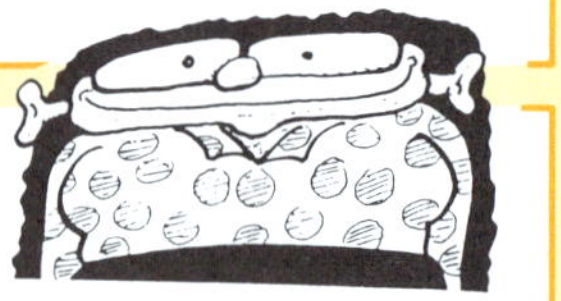

Follow-up

- Children write short descriptions of things around them, at home and at school and discuss the adjectives they have used with a friend. Can the friend help them to think of even better adjectives?
- Most children learn about comparison of adjectives in the way that they learn most language: through subconscious assimilation and use. However, when confusion arises, it is worth setting out the comparisons in table form to make the correct usage clear.

POSITIVE	COMPARATIVE	SUPERLATIVE
big	*bigger*	*biggest*
happy	*happier*	*happiest*
good	*better*	*best*
little	*less*	*least*
beautiful	*more beautiful*	*most beautiful*
comfortable	*more comfortable*	*most comfortable*

- Make up matching games using the table. Put in exceptions to rules so children are aware there is no simple way of learning this.

Adjectives

Adjectives

An adjective is a describing word. It gives more information about a noun, e.g.

The ghost gave a **heavy** sigh.
The **little** girl hid under the bedclothes.
The house was **haunted.**

Work in pairs to fill the gaps with suitable adjectives.

Varney the Vampire climbed in through the ____________ window. He saw a ____________ four-poster bed where a ____________ girl was sleeping. He bared his ____________ teeth in a ____________ snarl and crept towards her. He paused to admire her beauty. She had ____________ hair, her ____________ eyes were ____________, her lips were ____________ but above all her neck was ____________ . Varney leaned over and sank his fangs into her ________ skin. She let out a ____________ scream, but it was too late.

NOW Work in pairs to describe this picture. Use adjectives to make your description as vivid as possible.

The Adjective Game - Ideas Page

Activity

- Before playing the game, children will need to know the basics about adjectives (see page 14).
- Children play in pairs. They are asked to imagine that police are trying to identify a gang of criminals from verbal descriptions only, given by their victims before they died. An 'identity parade' of suspects is held. In order to make the 'identity parade' fair, the criminals have to be identified by their descriptions rather than by their appearances. The game is played as follows:

  Each player has a sheet of character cards which are cut out before the game begins.

  1. Players begin by writing four adjectives on the back of each card to describe the character on the front.
  2. Player 1 then selects a card, and without letting player 2 see the card, reads out the adjectives which he/she has written on the back. If he/she uses sentences or any kind of words other than adjectives, player 2 wins the card.
  3. Player 2 then guesses which character is being described. If he/she is correct, he/she wins the card and the criminal is handed over for trial!
  4. If the guess is incorrect, the card is laid aside. Perhaps the person is innocent, perhaps the description was not good enough. In any case, there is insufficient evidence and the person is set free.
- The level of difficulty can be raised by allowing children to use fewer adjectives to describe each character and/or by adding a second sheet of characters which have only minor differences from the first. This can be done by photocopying the original sheet and making slight modifications with correction fluid and a black pen.

Follow-up

- Children can choose the card they liked best, mount it on a sheet of paper and write a description to go with it. The description can be either a factual report, e.g. a police report, or an imaginative description, e.g. a scene from a story.
- Another alternative is to ask children to discuss the story behind the identity parade, e.g. What was the crime? How did the victims die? and thus build up a complete story which they could write collaboratively.
- Describing objects can be difficult for children. Try using a table at first to add vocabulary.

shape	size	colour	texture
	big		*rough*

- This also gives children an opportunity to use a thesaurus to build up as many adjectives as they can. Discussions can follow as to the subtle differences in meaning which words give, e.g. what is the difference between frumpish and dishevelled, untidy and scruffy, beautiful and elegant?
- Look at advertisements in newspapers and magazines. What kinds of adjectives do they use and why?

The Adjective Game

Adjective Poems - Ideas Page

Background

Writing poetry is the ideal way to explore the creative use of adjectives. Short forms like the haiku, or the one adjective poems, have the effect of making each word count. The use of space, especially in lines two and three, also emphasises the adjectives.

Activity

Children will enjoy reading these poems to each other. They could also be asked to pick out the adjectives and to suggest others.

- The poems are based on a simple pattern which uses three adjectives. Part of the fun in writing the poems is the element of surprise about where the adjectives will appear.
- Here is a simple computer program based on the same principle. It is written in a standard version of the international computer language, BASIC, which should work on most machines. Simply type in the program exactly as it is written, remembering to press RETURN at the end of every line:

```
  5 REM ***Adjective Poem***
 10 CLS
 20 PRINT  "Type in a noun-"
 25 INPUT  A$
 30 PRINT  "An adjective to describe your noun-"
 35 INPUT  B$
 40 PRINT  "Another-"
 45 INPUT  C$
 50 PRINT  "And another-"
 55 INPUT  D$
 60 PRINT  "Write a phrase describing what your noun looks like-"
 65 INPUT  E$
 70 PRINT  "Here is your poem..."
 75 PRINT
 90 PRINT  A$
100 PRINT  D$
110 PRINT  C$
120 PRINT  E$
130 PRINT  "The ";B$;" ";A$
140 END
```

Follow-up

- Children work in pairs. When they have written a poem they can swap and try to find different adjectives for each others' poems. Then they can discuss a final version. This encourages children to evaluate the effect of words very carefully. For example, the first poem on the sheet might be rewritten as follows:

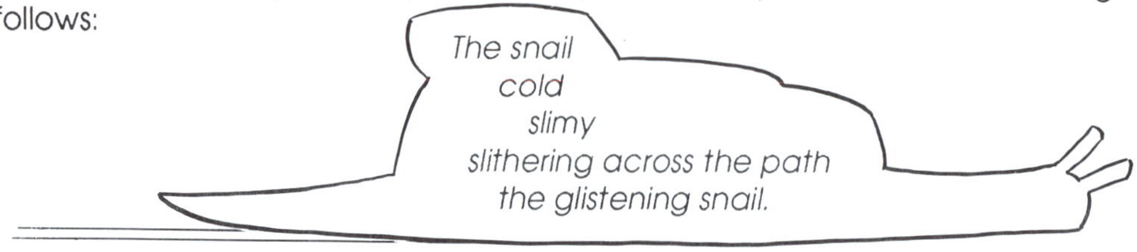

- These poems can be displayed within shapes or made into shape books for display.
- Writing poems to a set pattern has many advantages. Above all, it gives children a framework within which to write. However, it can be restrictive. They should therefore be encouraged to expand on their best poems in any way they like. For example, the emphasis on adjectives could be continued or a different emphasis such as rhyme could be introduced. Above all, the imagination should be allowed to take over from considerations of form and grammar.

Adjective Poems

Here are two poems. Take it in turns to read them to your partner.

The Robin
chirpy
friendly
looking for worms to eat
the pretty robin

The ghost
transparent
frightening
flitting around my bedroom
the lonely ghost

- Write your own adjective poems.

Think of a subject and write it on the first line, e.g.

The robin

- Now think of three adjectives to describe the robin and write them on three slips of paper. Fold and shuffle the papers. Miss two lines on the page.

On the fourth line write a phrase describing something the robin does, e.g.

looking for worms to eat

Leave a space before robin on the last line, e.g.

the __________ robin

NOW

- Place your adjectives in the spaces so that the poem looks like the examples. Read it to your partner. Is there a better order for the adjectives?

Background

- A pronoun substitutes for a noun, thereby avoiding a great deal of unnecessary repetition. There are eight kinds of pronouns: personal, interrogative, indefinite, relative, demonstrative, reciprocal, reflexive and intensive, but the activity sheet only covers one, personal pronouns. The main teaching points for junior age children are as follows:
  - *the ability to recognise pronouns (initially personal pronouns only)*
  - *using pronouns to avoid unnecessary repetition*
  - *understanding the difference between first person and third person narrative*
  - *avoiding gender bias in using the third person pronoun.*
- Note that, although the personal pronouns have been grouped according to case, (column one - subjective case; column two - objective case; column three - possessive case,) these terms have not been used on the activity sheet and should not be taught to any but the most able children. Generally speaking, children know which case to use, and attempting to teach theabstract and difficult concept of case is more likely to cause confusion than clarify it. Any problems, perhaps resulting from local dialect forms, should be dealt with individually.

Activity

- Some of the repetitions in the passage are so obvious as to be humorous. Children will easily recognise and correct these. However when these are dealt with, there remain the subtler choices. For example, many of the sentences contain Trevor's name. Is it most effective to change all but the first to pronouns, or to leave at least one more in? An immediate follow-up to this exercise should be for children to look over a recent piece of their own writing to see how they have used pronouns.
- What is **first** and **third person**? The best way to help pupils understand this is to conjugate a simple verb in full, e.g.

	singular	**plural**
first person:	I sing	we sing
second person:	you sing	you sing
third person:	he/she/it sings	they sing

Further work on verbs may be found on page 22-23.

- **Third Person Problems.** The problem posed by the exercise is a common one. There is a choice of solutions:
- write 'he or she'
- use one of the new pronouns made up for the purpose: 'he/she'.
- rewrite the passage to avoid the problem - e.g. by using the plural ('When children come to St. Thomas's School they ...').

Follow-up

- A story can be written from either the first person or third person point of view. A story written in the first person narrative would use the pronoun 'I' and a story written in the third person would use the pronouns 'he' or 'she'.
  In case there is any doubt, children should be shown an example of a story written in the first person and a story written in the third person. They should then discuss what kind of story each is suitable for, i.e. first person narrative is best for telling a story from a personal point of view. This should be followed by writing their own stories in order to experiment with both.
- **Adventure Game Stories.** It is unusual to find stories written in the second person, but adventure game stories are a good example. The reader is the hero of the adventure. Give children (perhaps working in pairs or small groups) this beginning as an example. They can then complete it, or make up one of their own.

  You are walking in the country when a sudden storm blows up. Nearby is an old deserted house. It looks spooky, but at least it is dry ...

Pronouns

Pronouns

A pronoun is used in place of a noun, e.g.

Trevor has a new computer. He likes to play games on it.

Here is a complete list of personal pronouns:

1st person 2nd person 3rd person	singular singular singular	I you he/she/it	me you him/her/it	my, mine your, yours his/hers/its
1st person 2nd person 3rd person	plural plural plural	we you they	us you them	our, ours your, yours their, theirs

- Change some of the nouns for pronouns to cut down the repetition in this passage.

Trevor received a new computer for Christmas. Trevor had also got two games for Trevor's computer. Trevor couldn't wait to try the games. First of all Trevor put the 'Space Attack' disk in, but the disk would not load. Trevor tried the other disk but the other disk would not load either. Trevor was furious. Just then, Trevor's dad came into the room. Trevor told Trevor's dad that the games wouldn't load, and Trevor's dad looked carefully at the games. Suddenly Trevor's dad laughed. "These games are for a different make of computer. Never mind, I'll change these games tomorrow!"

NOW

- Read this extract from a school booklet.

When your child comes to St. Thomas's School he will learn the basic skills of reading, writing and numeracy. He will need a pair of plimsolls for P.E. and a schoolbag for his books and pencils. It will be helpful if all his clothes have name labels. We hope your child will be happy at St. Thomas's School.

But there are boys and girls at St. Thomas's! Can you rewrite it so that the girls do not feel left out?

Verbs - Ideas Page

Background

- A verb is the most complex part of speech: the *Collins English Grammar* devotes over a hundred pages to explaining it. It would be impossible to teach such complexity to junior age children, so selectivity is important. Appropriate aims for younger juniors (and perhaps less able older children) are:
  - to know a simple definition of 'verb'
  - to understand the difference between present and past tense and that regular verbs form the past tense by adding -ed. (Of course, the tense system in English is much more complex than this)
  - to be able to recognise verbs in their own writing and in the books they read.

Activity

- **Varney the Vampire.** This activity gives children the chance to practise the skills they have just learned. Note that at this stage it does not matter if they do not recognise all the verbs or if they miss out some auxiliary verbs, or parts of phrasal verbs. At this stage the important thing is that children understand the general idea.

Follow-up

- The activity should be followed up by a similar activity based on children's own work and reading.
- More able children will benefit from the follow-up activities which ask them to look more carefully at the verbs they have underlined.
- When the children have read about what Varney the Vampire did, ask them to write about what they did yesterday evening. They can then swap their work and look for the same things that they looked for in the Varney passage.
- Explain to the children that verbs change slightly according to whether they are singular or plural, or which person (I, you, he/she/it, etc.) they refer to and give them some examples:

Infinitive:	**To love**	
Present Tense	**Singular**	**Plural**
First person:	I love	We love
Second person:	You love	You love
Third person:	He/she/it loves	They love
Past (simple) Tense	**Singular**	**Plural**
First person:	I loved	We loved
Second person:	You loved	You loved
Third person:	He/she/it loved	They loved

- Ask children to choose some of the verbs they have underlined and write them out in full in both present and past tenses.
- Finally, it is well worth asking them to write out the verbs *'To have'* and *'To be'* in both past and present tense. Why not make a wall display of them? This will help children to avoid mistakes such as 'we was'.
- To consolidate the idea of verb tenses, use the idea of weather forecasting. Collect together forecasts for the next week and ask children to role play giving a TV or radio forecast. They will soon become aware that they are using the future tense. Now ask children to role play yesterday's forecast (making suitable apologies for getting it wrong!) to give them an awareness of the past tense.

Verbs

Verbs

A verb is a doing word. It tells what people, animals or things do.

The teacher opens the door.

The choirboys sing sweetly.

The night grows cold.

The sun is shining.

These examples are all in the present tense. They tell us about things that are happening now.

Most verbs form their past tense by adding -ed. For example, if the teacher had opened the door yesterday, the sentence would read:

The teacher opened his door.

Verbs which end in -ed in the past tense are called regular verbs. Verbs which form their past tense differently, such as sing, sang or grow, grew are called irregular verbs .

- Underline the verbs in this passage. If you are not sure, ask yourself 'What did Varney do?'

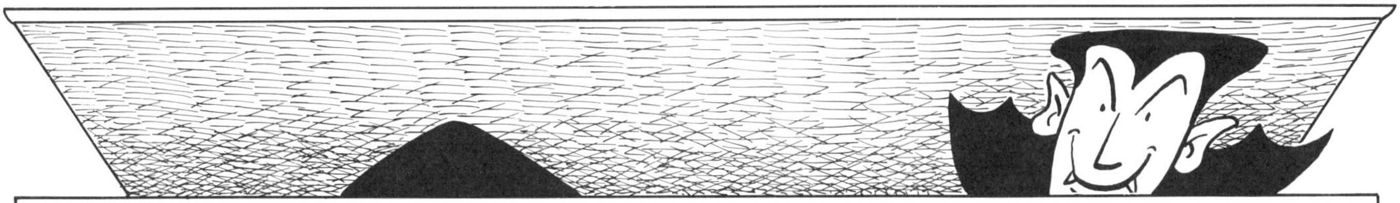

Varney the Vampire pushed open the coffin lid and sat up slowly. He rubbed his eyes and groaned. He felt hungry for another feast of blood. Suddenly he changed into a bat and flew to the castle where someone was sleeping. He flew in through the open window and changed back into his human form. He smiled. There was not one, but three people sleeping in the room. It was his lucky night!

NOW Look again at the passage about Varney the Vampire.

- Are the verbs in the present or past tense?
- Which are regular and which are irregular verbs?

Background

- An adverb is often called 'the dustbin part of speech' because of the tendency of grammarians to dump in it anything that will not fit elsewhere. It is unnecessary to enter into all the complexities of adverb use when teaching junior children. The main aims are that children should:
  - know and understand a simple definition
  - be able to recognise adverbs with **-ly** endings and understand their relationship with verbs
  - be aware that some adverbs do not have **-ly** endings
  - and most important of all, be able to use adverbs creatively in their own writing.
- Note that it is important for children to be able to recognise nouns and verbs because they are the 'anchor points' of a sentence, e.g. in redrafting a piece of writing, children may need to find a verb in order to improve the description by adding an adverb. It is less important that they are able to recognise and name all the different kinds of adverb. However, more able pupils could usefully explore the traditional categories: adverbs of Time, Place, Manner and Degree. The examples on the resource sheet have been grouped in this way, though the groups have not been labelled to avoid confusion The **-ly** adverbs are adverbs of Manner, and the other adverbs are set out on three lines, giving examples of adverbs of Time, Place and Degree.

Activities

- The first activity gives practice in recognition, mainly of **-ly** adverbs. This should be followed by practice in recognition of adverbs in children's own writing and in their reading books.
- The second activity is a cloze exercise. Children fill the gaps with **-ly** adverbs. Place the emphasis here on selecting the most appropriate and imaginative adverbs.

Follow-up

- Children can work in pairs to redraft a piece of writing. This follow-up is particularly important because it teaches children to use their knowledge of adverbs as a tool to improve their writing.
- They will need to find all the verbs first and then discuss if any improvement is needed. If they decide to add an adverb, they should be encouraged to read a few sentences before and after the sentence that is being changed, to make sure they understand the precise meaning, in the context of the surrounding sentences. Use of the thesaurus should be encouraged.
- **The Adverb game.** This game is played in pairs. Player 1 says 'What are you going to do on Saturday?' Player 2 must reply with one word - a verb, e.g. 'swim'. Player 1 then asks 'How?' Player 2 replies with an adverb, e.g. 'quickly.'
- Many adjectives can be made into adverbs simply by adding **-ly**. Give children a list to experiment with:

quick	**sudden**	**brief**
brave	**awkward**	**willing**
quiet	**accidental**	**heavy**
loud	**slow**	**foolish**
cruel	**happy**	**hasty**
bad	**angry**	**greedy**

- Children can make an Adverb Spinner. Make it from two circles of card joined in the centre. The outside circle is larger and has **-ly** endings written on it. The smaller inside circle has adjectives written on it. Move the outside circle to match up with the adverbs, e.g. bad = badly. Talk about which adverb endings are correct.

Adverbs

Adverbs

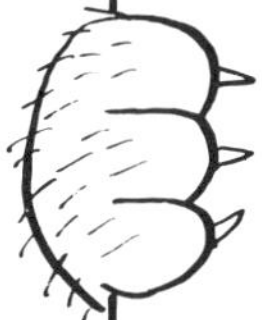

Adverbs describe verbs. They give us more information. In the sentence 'The wolf ran quickly', 'ran' is the verb, and 'quickly' is the adverb which tells us HOW the wolf ran.

Many adverbs are formed from adjectives by adding -ly, e.g.

ADJECTIVE		ADVERB
happy	→	happily
graceful	→	gracefully
awkward	→	awkwardly
sad	→	sadly

OTHER ADVERBS

before, soon, now, already, since, here, there, everywhere, nowhere, almost, rather, very, much, only, quite.

- Underline the adverbs in this passage.

He ran quickly down the street. He looked anxiously left and right. Fortunately everything was quiet. He felt tired and rather unhappy to be running away so soon. He reached the crossroads and stopped. He started again and turned into the High Street. Suddenly he stopped. There was the sound of footsteps behind him. His heart beat violently. He was being followed!

- Use -ly adverbs to fill the gaps in this passage.

The fishing boat floated ___________ on the calm ocean. Then Hal saw a black fin moving ___________. It was a shark. He took the oar, and beat the shark ___________ on the head. The shark thrashed the water ___________. Hal hit it again and the shark sank ___________ from sight. Hal sat down ___________.

Background

- A sentence is one of the most difficult units of language to define. Over a hundred different definitions have been offered - most of them too complicated for teaching purposes. What we must aim for as teachers is to build up the concept of sentences for our children over an extended period. For example, we might begin with:

  A sentence is a group of words that begins with a capital letter and ends with a full stop. It makes sense on its own.

  Later we might introduce some grammatical terms into our definition:

  A sentence must contain a verb.

- These definitions would become more complex and above all would be reinforced by the look and feel of thousands of real examples in children's own reading and writing.

Activities

- Children adapt the outline on the resource sheet to look like themselves. They write some sentences describing themselves using the sentence patterns suggested, as well as any others they can think of.
- The next step is to look for pairs of sentences that can be joined together with 'and'. Statements joined by 'and' should be connected in some way, e.g. 'I have a blue anorak and grey trousers,' (clothes); 'I have blue eyes and lots of freckles,' (face).
- Each child should now have a selection of longer sentences. The next step is to put these together with the remaining shorter sentences in the most effective order.
- Do not worry if the end product sounds rather wooden as this is part of a gradual learning process.
- Finally, they could be asked to write freely about themselves. There will be some subconscious carry-over of sentence patterns and the previous exercise can be referred to in discussions.

Follow-up

Below are some general strategies which have been found useful in teaching the basics of writing in sentences:

- Encourage children to read their work aloud to each other and to you. Teach them to listen to the falling intonation that marks the end of a sentence.
- Occasionally discuss sentences when hearing children read, or when reading to small groups.
- Establish some simple parameters.
  A sentence begins with a capital letter and ends with a full stop.
  It tells you about one or two things.
  Limit the number of 'ands' to one per sentence.
  It is important to tell children that these are guides only.
- **How to bath a dog.** Explaining simple procedures clearly can make children aware of the importance of sentences. Ask groups to work out steps necessary to perform a simple action, e.g. How to bath a dog. When they are listed, they need to be sequenced correctly. Children can read out their simple instructions to others to decide just how clear they are. Ask questions such as, 'Would using joining words such as 'next' or 'then' make the sentence flow more easily?' 'Would the audience understand the instructions better?'

Sentences

Sentences

A sentence is a group of words that begins with a capital letter and ends with a full stop, question or exclamation mark, e.g.

I am eight years old.

Make this outline look like you and fill in the gaps.

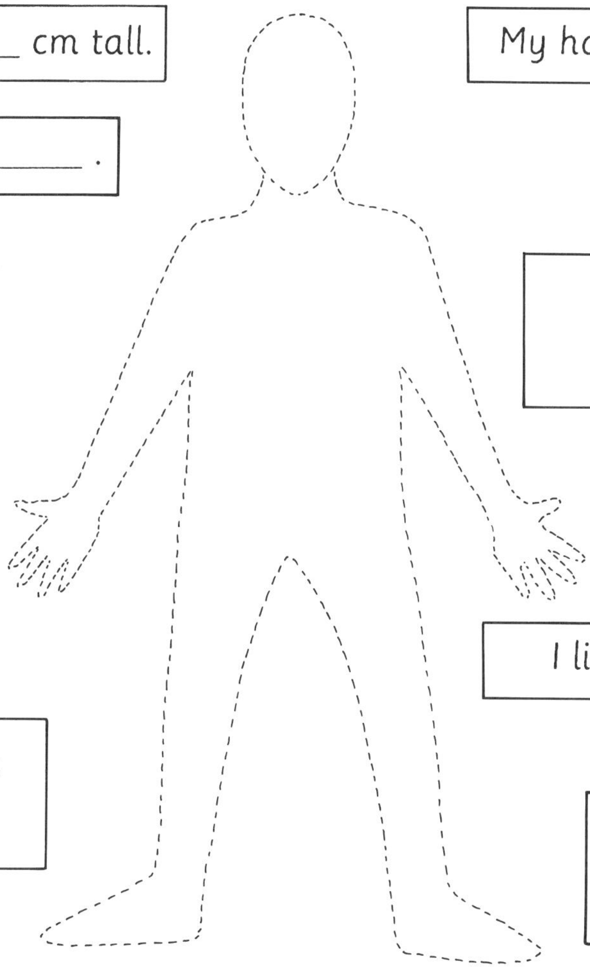

I am ______ m ______ cm tall.

My eyes are __________ .

I am __________ .

My best friend is __________ .

My favourite food is __________ .

My hair is __________ .

I am wearing __________ .

I like __________ .

My shoes are __________ .

NOW ● Write more sentences about yourself.

Continue over the page ...

Sentence Building 1 - Ideas Page

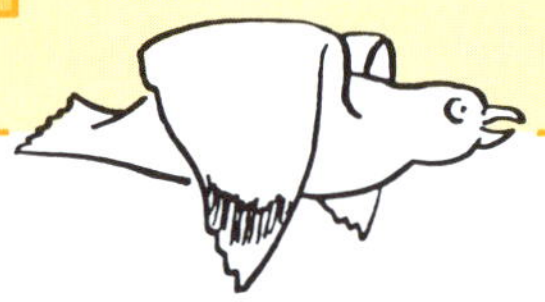

Background

- When children are becoming confident about writing in sentences they are ready for the next step, i.e. how to make their sentences more interesting and varied. The easiest way to do this is to add adjectives and adverbs.

Activity

- The activity sheet introduces children to the idea of developing a sentence by adding one or two adjectives. When they have mastered this, the same idea can be extended to adverbs.
- There are no correct answers to the sentences given. Many different adjectives will work equally well. To begin with it may help to restrict children to the adjectives listed to ensure that the words they use to extend the sentences are actually adjectives. When they have acquired the 'feel' of this, they will be ready to add adjectives of their own.
- The activity can be developed in a 'fun' way by playing the following game. The words, along with any other words added by children, are cut up, folded, and placed in a pile in the middle of the table. Children play in pairs. They take it in turns to select words at random. The child can place the words in any sentence and can move them around as the game goes on. The first to fill all the gaps and create sentences that make sense is the winner.
- The value of this game is that it generates some unexpected and thought-provoking combinations which counteracts the tendency of most gap-filling exercises to produce clichés, e.g.

  Instead of 'The lonely dog barked at the silvery moon', children might write 'The thoughtful dog barked at the dusty moon'.

  These lines could be discussed. Why is the dog thoughtful? Why is the moon dusty? A poem or story might develop from the discussion.
- A further development is to ask children to add another adjective (plus comma) to the first noun, for example: 'The angry, exasperated teacher glared at the naughty schoolgirl.'

Follow-up

- Draw attention to the use of adjectives in books children are reading and when reading aloud take the opportunity to discuss how the writer has used adjectives to make descriptions more accurate and interesting.
- This can occasionally be done in a more formal way by asking children to underline adjectives in a selected passage photocopied on to a piece of paper.
- When children are fully confident with the idea of stretching a sentence by adding adjectives, it can be taken further by teaching them to add adverbs (see page 42) in the same way. The same sentences could be used as a basis, e.g.

Sentence: The shark gnawed at the boat.
Add adjectives: The hungry shark gnawed at the little boat.
Add an adverb: The hungry shark gnawed viciously at the little boat.

Sentence Building

Add an Adjective

A sentence can often be made more interesting by adding an adjective or two.

The [girl] (noun) drank the [water.] (noun)

This sentence can be improved by adding adjectives to the two nouns.

The [thirsty] (adjective) girl drank the [cool] (adjective) water.

- Add adjectives to the sentences. You can choose words from the word box below, or choose your own.

The teacher smiled at the schoolgirl.

____

The dog barked at the moon.

____

The shark gnawed at the boat.

____

The car roared along the road.

____

The tramp rested in the house.

____

The bus reversed into the van.

____

WORD BOX

winding	neglected	fragile	silvery	freshly-painted	green
timid	distant	vicious	thoughtful	tired	weary
bloodthirsty	hungry	new	dilapidated	old	haunted
lonely	dusty	shining	sports	red	removal

Description Builders - Ideas Page

Activity

- The sentence building ideas in the activity sheet on page 29 can be explored more fully and more creatively using 'description builder' poems. The preset pattern and gradual build up gives children plenty of support to begin with. Later they can use the patterns more freely and even invent their own patterns. They should read the example, then use the blank pattern below to write their own. If children have difficulty getting started, make a game of it. Use the noun cards from page 13, form children into small groups and ask each child to select a card at random. He/she then has to write a description builder poem based upon it. Finally, children read out their description builders to each other.
- Below is another approach in the form of a short computer program. Children will enjoy experimenting with the endless variations the program can produce and the public nature of the monitor screen will encourage them to write collaboratively. The program is written in a standard version of BASIC and only needs typing in.

```
10  REM****SUPER SENTENCE
    MARKER****C.WEBSTER****
20  CLS
30  S$ = " "
40  P$ = " "
50  PRINT "Write the noun which
    your sentence is about -"
60  INPUT A$
70  PRINT "Write an adjective
    to describe your noun -"
80  INPUT B$
90  PRINT "Write another
    adjective -"
100 INPUT C$
110 PRINT "Write a verb to say
    what your noun is doing -"
120 INPUT E$
130 PRINT "Write an adverb to
    describe the verb -"
140 INPUT F$
150 PRINT "Complete the phrase
    'Looking like...'
160 INPUT G$
170 PRINT
180 PRINT "Here are two
    versions of your super
    sentence."
190 PRINT "Choose the one you
    like best."
200 PRINT
210 PRINT "The "; C$; P$; S$;
    B$; S$; A$; S$;
220 PRINT E$; S$; F$; P$; S$;
    " looking like "; G$; "."
230 PRINT
240 PRINT " Looking like "; G$;
     P$; S$; " the "; B$; P$;
250 PRINT S$; C$; S$; A$; S$;
    E$; S$; F$; "."
260 END
```

Follow-up

- Although these poems start out as patterns designed to reinforce knowledge of grammar, their creative potential should not be underestimated. However, to bring out this potential, teacher and child should be prepared to:
  - add to the basic poem produced by the set pattern
  - depart from the set pattern where something else would be more effective
  - exploit the freedom to experiment that poetry makes possible.
- Think of other patterns for 'description builder' poems; for example, see the adjective poems on page 19. Another idea is to include some 'looks like' lines to build up imaginative comparisons.

  For example:

  The rock
  The large rock
  The large grey rock
  LOOKS LIKE my grandad's
  rugged face and grey hair.

  Or:

  The large, grey, jagged rock rolled lumbering down the steep, slippery mountain LIKE a 17-tonne lorry thundering down the road.
- Ask groups of children to write their own descriptions of stories they have read. Use three large cards:
  - describe the main character
  - describe an episode in the book
  - describe the setting of the story

  and add others if required.
  Hang these as a mobile with suitable illustrations.

Description Builders

Write a short poem in which description is built up following a set pattern.

Begin with a noun: The rock

Add an adjective: The large rock
Add another: The large, grey rock
And another: The large, grey, jagged rock
Add a verb: The large, grey, jagged rock rolled
Add an adverb: The large, grey, jagged rock rolled lumberingly
Add an ending: The large, grey, jagged rock rolled lumberingly down the mountain
Add an adjective to the ending: The large, grey, jagged rock rolled lumberingly down the steep mountain
Add another: The large, grey, jagged rock rolled lumberingly down the steep, slippery mountain.

NOW Try it yourself:

Begin with a noun: ______________________

Add an adjective: ______________________

Add another: ______________________

And another: ______________________

Add a verb: ______________________

Add an adverb: ______________________

Add an ending: ______________________

Add an adjective to the ending: ______________________

Add another: ______________________

A Thank You Letter - Ideas Page

Activity

- This activity makes use of the idea of substitutional grammar, but in a lighthearted way. This can reinforce children's growing awareness of the parts of speech and how they are combined to make sentences. It also helps children understand the idea that a part of speech is a 'slot' in a sentence that can be filled by a word, phrase or clause.
- The activity sheet can be used in a number of ways:
  - It can be used as a serious exercise in substitutional grammar in which children choose words from the list to compose a letter that makes sense. There are five choices in each list, plus 'other' which invites children to choose their own word or phrase.
  - It can be used in a fun way. Children roll dice to select the word or phrase which is then entered in the slot. Whenever a six is rolled, they have to make up their own word or phrase. When a small group of children has played in this way, they will have great fun reading out the resulting letters to each other!
  - The real challenge comes in designing something similar. A holiday postcard is a simple option, but the same idea can be used for lots of things, e.g. a school 'excuse note', a poem, or even a story.

Follow-up

- Children will also enjoy and learn from another popular game based on substitutional grammar - The Curse Generator.
- The game is played in groups of four.
- Each child writes *may your* and a *noun* on a piece of paper without letting anyone else see. The paper is folded to hide what has been written and passed on to the next person.
- Each child now adds a *verb* to the paper he/she has just received and so on, until all four columns are complete.
- The process goes on until each paper has been round several times. The papers are then unfolded and the curses read out. Any uncertainty about grammatical terms can be avoided by giving children a sample curse which they can use as a model.

- As ever, the child who reads avidly will assimilate unconsciously more complex sentence patterns. So continue to encourage reading, reading and more reading!
- **Cloze procedure in poems.** Write poems using only adjectives and nouns - two adjectives and one noun per line. The poem can have any number of lines.

  Shallow, clear sea,
  Tired, sleepy diver
  Swift, ferocious shark ...

  Blank out nouns and adjectives. Ask children to identify what part of speech is missing and replace it with a suitable word. Children can discuss the different effects created.

A Thank You Letter

Use this sheet to help you write a Thank You letter. Simply fill in the gaps using the wordlists.

Dear ____A____ ,

Thank you for the ____B____ ____C____ which you sent me

for ____D____. I will ____E____ it ____F____, and I

____G____ it will remind me of the ____H____ times we had

last ____I____.

I hope you liked the ____J____ which I sent you.

Hoping to see you ____K____

Yours ____L____,

A. Proper Noun

1. Gran
2. Uncle
3. Mavis
4. Father Christmas
5. Cousin
6. Other

B. Adjective

1. lovely
2. useful
3. beautiful
4. unusual
5. magnificent
6. Other

C. Noun

1. fishing rod
2. pet
3. personal organiser
4. jigsaw puzzle
5. trampoline
6. Other

D. Proper Noun/Noun

1. Christmas
2. Easter
3. my birthday
4. a get well present
5. a joke
6. Other

E. Verb

1. treasure
2. keep
3. use
4. worry about
5. hide
6. Other

F. Adverb

1. always
2. sometimes
3. proudly
4. carefully
5. awkwardly
6. Other

G. Verb

1. know
2. hope
3. trust
4. dare say
5. fear
6. Other

H. Adjective

1. happy
2. interesting
3. special
4. joyful
5. boring
6. Other

I. Noun

1. summer
2. spring
3. autumn
4. winter
5. holiday
6. Other

J. Noun

1. chocolates
2. flowers
3. dinner service
4. fishtank
5. cactus
6. Other

K. Adverb

1. soon
2. next week
3. before long
4. never
5. next year
6. Other

L. Close

1. truly
2. faithfully
3. sincerely
4. with loving kisses
5. with regards
6. Other

Sentence Building 2 - Ideas Page

Background

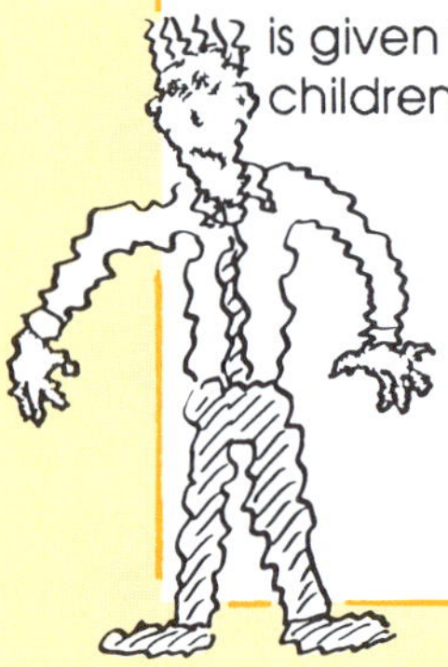

- Conjunctions join parts of a sentence. There are two types: **co-ordinating** and **subordinating**. There are only three co-ordinating conjunctions: **and**, **or**, **but**. These join clauses or parts of clauses with equal weight. There are many more subordinating conjunctions. Below a fuller list is given than on the activity sheet. Extra conjunctions from this list can be introduced as children become more confident:

after	*while*	*supposing*	*because*
as	*where*	*although*	*for*
before	*wherever*	*though*	*to*
since	*unless*	*if*	*so that*
until	*in case*	*whereas*	*like*
when	*as long as*	*except*	*so*

Activities

- The reason for studying conjunctions is to help children to see that there are several ways of combining two statements, each way with its own emphasis. The first step is to help children to generate a list of possibilities from any two statements - like the examples in the template. It is important to stress that:
  - some pairs of statements can only be joined in one or possibly two ways
  - some pairs of statements can be joined in several ways
  - children must use their common sense to avoid clumsy or ungrammatical joining statements (though be prepared for quite a few of these during the early stages of learning and experimentation!).
- The second step is to encourage children to discuss the fine differences in meaning and emphasis. This can be done most effectively when the statements are placed in a context. One way to do this is to take a short passage from a story and blank out a suitable sentence, which can be presented (perhaps in a modified form) as two statements, for children to work on and discuss.

Follow-up

- A simple way to encourage children to use more conjunctions is simply to ask for a more detailed description. This often generates more interesting sentences, including the use of conjunctions and subordinate clauses, without the pain of learning new terminology.
- Write the list of conjunctions on cards and ask children to shuffle them and pick one out at random. They then have to invent a sentence which uses that conjunction. In doing this they will have fun and make some silly mistakes, but also generate some perfectly correct subordinate clauses.
- Children should be encouraged to apply this knowledge to their own writing. At the redrafting stage the teacher or writing partner could suggest sentences to experiment with, e.g.
  - When too many statements have been joined with 'and'.
  - When there are too many short sentences, some of which could be effectively joined by conjunctions.
  - When a simple co-ordinating conjunction has been used, but the sentence could be made more effective by using a subordinating conjunction.

Sentence Building

Conjunctions

Conjunctions are joining words. The commonest conjunctions are:

and, but, where, as, when, although, because, while, until.

They are used to join statements together.

Two statements:	He changed into a wolf. The moon was full.
Joined:	The moon was full **and** he changed into a wolf.
Or:	**When** the moon was full, he changed into a wolf.
Or:	He changed into a wolf **because** the moon was full.
Or:	**Because** the moon was full, he changed into a wolf.
Or:	He changed into a wolf **while** the moon was full.

NOW

- Take each pair of statements and use conjunctions to join them together in as many different ways as make sense.

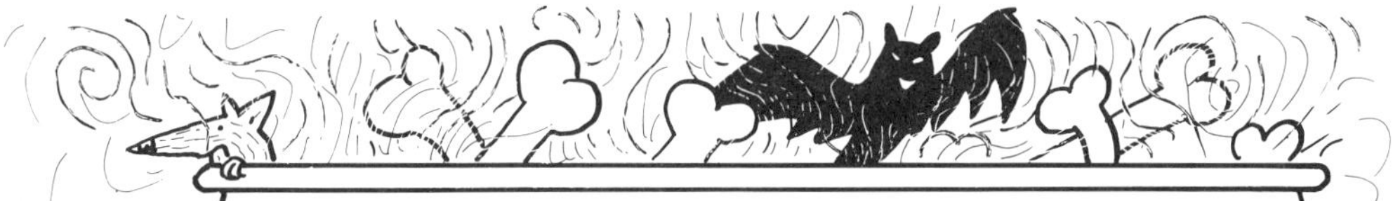

Dracula bared his fangs. Chris fainted.

It was dark. The ghost glowed faintly.

Surinder had a strong crowbar.

The coffin was tightly sealed.

I turned out the light. I saw something strange.

The witch offered me some soup. I did not want it.

I thought it was a bird. It fluttered strangely.

- Joining the statements in different ways makes a slight difference to the meaning. Talk about the different meanings of sentences you have written.

Sentence Building 3 - Ideas Page

Background

- The phrase in apposition is a common way of expanding a sentence, making it more interesting to the reader.

Activity

- The activity sheet begins with a template which is followed by simple practice exercises. The follow-up exercise is designed to help children transfer their new knowledge to their own writing. Do not be too concerned if they do this clumsily at first. Like any new skill, it takes time to internalise and eventually it should take its place in their repertoire of writing.

Follow-up

- If progression from the activity sheet to children using phrases in apposition in their own work is too great, the following intermediate exercises can be used:
  1. Give children a short story or description in which gaps are left for phrases in apposition and ask them to complete them in pairs.
  2. Give children a similar passage but without gaps. They then have to identify suitable points to add phrases in apposition.
- Phrases in apposition are particularly useful for giving a quick character description. Give children these examples:

  Marilyn Monroe, a famous film star, died in mysterious circumstances.
  Harold, the last Anglo-Saxon king, was killed at the battle of Hastings.
  Sandra, a tall, fair-haired girl, is my best friend.

- Children then compose sentences about their friends, relatives, favourite media personalities, etc. using the same pattern.
- Children should now be able to use phrases in apposition in their own writing. They may need reminding of this at first, e.g. by a redrafting checklist (see page 47), a writing partner, or the teacher, but the pattern will gradually become internalised and be used naturally.
- Ask children to look for phrases in apposition in the books they are reading. Better still, give them some short passages which have been chosen because they contain good examples. Like most points of grammar, it will need to be repeated a number of times over the junior phase. Children will gradually become familiar with the concept and begin to use phrases in apposition naturally.
- Take this opportunity to discuss other ways of 'breaking up' a sentence to investigate its composition, e.g. subjects and predicates. Teaching this important grammatical point does not have to be boring. Explain that the subject of a sentence is what it is about and that the predicate is the rest.
- Make two word strips labelled *subject* and *predicate*. Cut them out and place them side by side. Slide them up and down to create new sentences according to the definition just given.

Subject	Predicate
The vampire	is tapping on the door
Susan	quivered with horror

Sentence Building

Phrase in apposition

A phrase in apposition is a few words of extra explanation written in a sentence.

Snow White, friend of the seven dwarfs, used to live in this castle.

Note that:

- *the sentence would still make sense if the phrase in apposition were removed*
- *the phrase is marked off by two commas*
- *if the end of the phrase is also the end of the sentence, a full stop is used.*

- *Put the phrases in apposition in the correct sentences.*

Jonathan Harker, ______________________________, set out for Transylvania.

He approached the castle, ______________________________.

Igor, ______________________________, opened the door.

The door, ______________________________, groaned on its hinges.

Count Dracula, ______________________________, welcomed Jonathan.

They went down to the crypt, ______________________________.

Jonathan, ______________________________, plunged the stake in Dracula's heart.

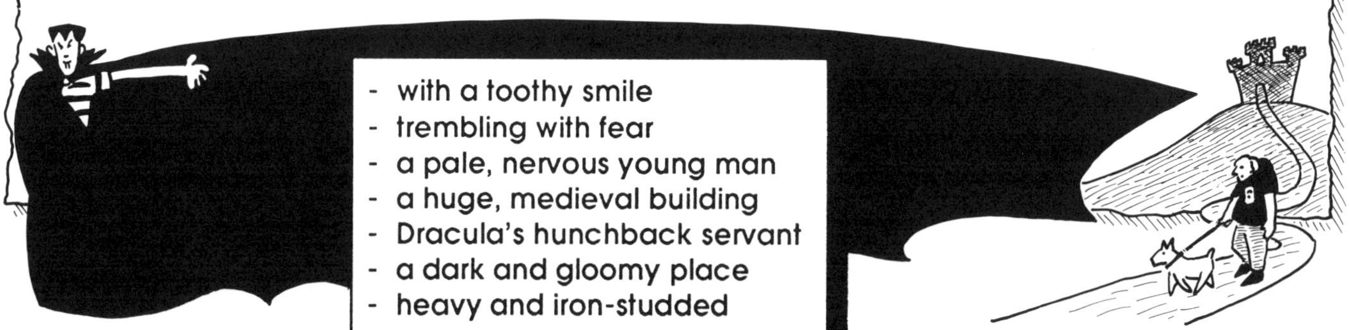

- **with a toothy smile**
- **trembling with fear**
- **a pale, nervous young man**
- **a huge, medieval building**
- **Dracula's hunchback servant**
- **a dark and gloomy place**
- **heavy and iron-studded**

NOW

- *Write your own version of the story of Count Dracula using some of the phrases above.*

Sentence Portraits - *Ideas Page*

Background

- Sentence portraits offer a structured way of exploring sentence variety. They also help to unlock children's creativity by asking them to describe a person in different ways.

Activity

- A good way to approach the activity on the photocopiable sheet is to ask children to work through the list of sentence ideas, missing out any that they find difficult. Some of the sentence ideas may need clarification, e.g.

3. **Write a very short sentence.**
   Stress that these must be complete sentences. A good way to help is to give the example of the shortest sentence in the Bible: 'Jesus wept'. This is the classic short sentence with a subject and verb.
8. **Write a very long sentence.**
   This must be one sentence, not several sentences strung together. Revise conjunctions (page 35) if necessary.
11. **Write a sentence with 'looks like' in it.**
   This is inviting pupils to write a simile. The term should be used with older and more able children.
12. **Write a sentence in which two or more words begin with the same sound.**
   This is inviting pupils to use alliteration. Again, the term should be used where appropriate.
14. **Write a sentence with two commas in it.**
   There are several ways to do this. The easiest ones are to write a list or to write a phrase in apposition (see page 37).

- The poem is a simple example of what the end product might look like. Encourage children to write more sentences and make them more interesting. A useful additional exercise is to ask the children which of the sentence ideas is used in each line.

Follow-up

- The activity sheet is mainly an exercise in sentence writing. However, the extension activity at the end of the sheet could be used to turn the sentences into a poem. A redrafting checklist is given to help (see page 47) but it should be stressed that children can adapt their work in any way they wish.
- Children could develop the sentences into a prose description. This is harder because ways have to be found to join the sentences in a logical sequence. The best advice is to ask children to write a simple description of their character and to work into this two or three of their best sentences from the activity.
- A similar structural approach can be used to guide writing about a range of subjects.

Sentence Portraits

Close your eyes and imagine a person that you know.
Now write a short sentence about that person, *e.g.*

He is my best friend.
or I've always liked the way you smile.

Add more sentences. Choose some ideas from the list below.

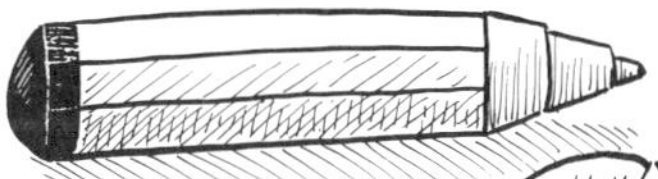

1. Write a sentence with a colour in it.
2. Write a sentence with a part of the body in it.
3. Write a very short sentence.
4. Write a sentence with 'because' in it.
5. Write a sentence that ends with an exclamation mark.
6. Write a sentence with a piece of clothing in it.
7. Write a sentence with an adjective and an adverb in it.
8. Write a very long sentence.
9. Write a sentence with 'but' in it.
10. Write a sentence with an animal in it.
11. Write a sentence with 'looks like' in it.
12. Write a sentence in which two or more words begin with the same sound.
13. Write a sentence with a question mark at the end.
14. Write a sentence with two commas in it.
15. Write a sentence with a wish in it.
16. Write a sentence with an emotion in it.

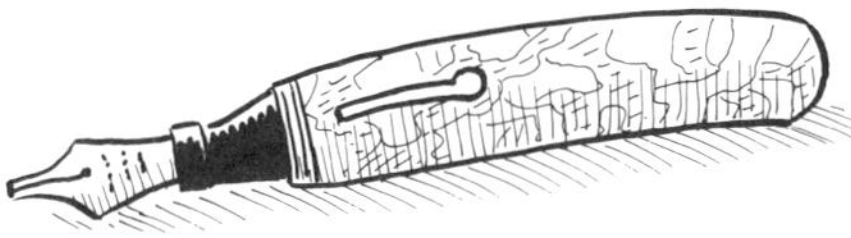

When you have finished you will have a poem something like this:

Susan was my friend.
Her hair was blonde.
She looked like my mother.
Her skin was soft and silky.
I really admired her.
I wish she was my friend now.

Redraft your poem by:
- making up a title
- adding more words or sentences
- taking out or changing anything that you do not like
- putting the sentences in a different order
- checking and rewriting your work.

How? Where? When? - Ideas Bank

Activity

- This activity is a complement to the series of activity sheets on sentence building (see pages 28, 34, 36). It is another way to achieve the same goal - it requires more detailed writing. Answering the questions will entail using adverbs, adjectives and subordinate clauses. The additional questions listed will invite more detail, explanation and the use of dialogue. The activity is meant to be fun, but its real application becomes obvious when children apply the technique to their own written work.

Follow-up

- Questioning techniques are useful to help children build up 'writing stamina', the ability to write at length. However, there are some children who need to do just the opposite - write shorter, less rambling pieces!
  They could be asked to develop just one scene of their stories using these techniques.
- It can also be a valuable way of helping children prepare to redraft their work. Asking these questions at the appropriate place in children's writing can help them to understand what else they need to do other than correct spelling and punctuation.
- This technique tends to teach an unconscious ability to write well and as such has its limitations. Ideally this method should be combined with the conscious study of grammar as outlined on previous pages.
- Try the same technique on a range of texts, e.g.
  - books for younger pupils
  - simple folk tales
  - ballads and narrative poems.

  It can also be used for non-fictional writing, e.g.
  - descriptions
  - newspaper reports
  - diary entries
  - science reports.

- These techniques can help children of all abilities. Children will benefit from working very closely with examples of detailed description from quality books. A bank of such descriptions is a useful classroom resource.
- These prompt questions could form an alternative Redrafting Checklist (see page 47), or an addition to the checklist. It is also worth making a poster to remind children of the prompt questions from the activity sheet.
- Take the opportunity to encourage children to distinguish between questions, statements and commands. One child can think of a list of instructions (commands), e.g.
  "Put the piece of wood in a vice."
  Another child asks a question; "Why do you do that?"
  The partner replies with a statement, "Because I need it to be steady."

How? Where? When?

Take it in turns to read each story aloud to your partner. When you have finished your partner should ask questions about the story. You must answer every question, even if you have to make up the answer!

Some questions to ask:

- How big ... ?
- What colour ... ?
- Can you tell me more about ... ?
- Why did he/she do that?
- What happened next?
- What was his/her name?
- What did he/she say?

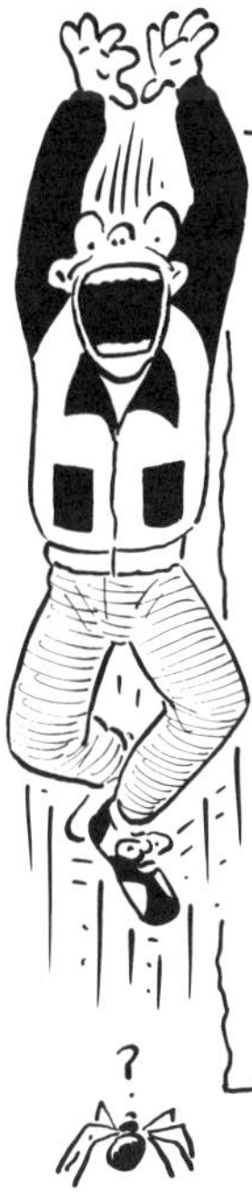

STORY NO 1.

Once there was a boy called James who was often being bullied at school. It was making his life a misery. There was one girl in particular who was always picking on him. One day the girl thumped him on the way home. That was enough! James decided to do something about it. He spent six weeks learning Judo. The next time the bully picked on him, he hit back and they had a fight. James lost. So much for karate! Then he decided to use brains where brawn had failed. He thought and he thought! Suddenly he remembered a science lesson where the bully had shown a weak spot. The next time she tried to pick on him, James was ready. He took out a matchbox in which he kept a spider. He threatened to throw the spider at the bully who pleaded for mercy as soon as she saw it. You see, she was scared stiff of creepy crawlies!

STORY NO 2.

Once there was a girl called Sarah who loved Christmas so much she wished that every day was Christmas Day. Luckily (or unluckily) a fairy (who just happened to be passing by) heard this wish and made it come true. To Sarah's delight, the next day was Christmas Day and she received lots of lovely presents. This went on and on until she had every present you could think of - and more besides, so it was not surprising that she was a little fed up with Christmas. Several weeks of Christmases passed, and then Sarah noticed something strange. She was getting very unsuitable presents like a walking stick and wrinkle cream and when she looked in the mirror she saw why. Every Christmas she had grown a year older! She was now a white-haired old lady! She screamed in horror and wished out loud that it would turn out to be a dream. Luckily the fairy was passing by again, and when Sarah woke up, she found it was!

Improving Dialogue - Ideas Page

Background

- The point of learning grammar is to write more effectively. These last activity sheets bring together several of the techniques covered earlier in this book in a way which will improve children's writing.

Activity

- Four points are discussed on the activity sheet. The writing of dialogue can be greatly improved by judicious application of a few of the simple techniques. Indeed, it is probably more difficult to punctuate and set out correctly than it is to use the three additional techniques.

1. **First of all**, it is important to ensure that children can set and punctuate dialogue correctly. The passage on the activity sheet is designed to remind children of the key points. Ask the children to copy the beginning of the story and write what happens next. They should include dialogue and set it out correctly. If this proves too difficult, it is likely that the rest of the sheet will be too difficult. In that case, they could usefully spend some time improving their punctuation of dialogue using simple examples.

2. **The second step** is to use some of the synonyms of 'said' for greater variety and precision. This can be prepared for in a number of ways:

- brainstorm the synonyms of 'said' and then consult a thesaurus
- make a large poster of a selection of these synonyms
- examine how 'real' writers use the synonyms of 'said'.

3. **The third step** is to add an adverb (see also the activity sheet on page 25). Again, brainstorming of suitable words and the use of a thesaurus will be a valuable preparation, especially as most of the adverbs will refer to different types of emotions.

4. **The fourth step** is to add a phrase of description (usually a participial phrase - an **-ing** phrase). Note that a participial phrase could be added to the sentence-building repertoire of more able children, both in this position and to begin a sentence.

Follow-up

- The passage on the activity sheet provides some practice in using the different techniques discussed on the activity sheet. It may well be that children will need more practice to become fully confident with these techniques. Indeed, they will continue to learn about this and other aspects of grammar well into their teens and beyond.
- The final result is that children will have a wide repertoire to draw on, ranging from using no 'said' phrases at all, to the ultimate described in step 4 and of course every possible combination, e.g. 'said' + adverb, or 'said' + phrase.
- The key to using such a repertoire effectively is artistic restraint. But be warned: just as the teacher with a new desktop publisher produces worksheets with ten different fonts per page, children are likely to go over the top at first. This will settle down, especially if children are encouraged to study dialogue in novels.

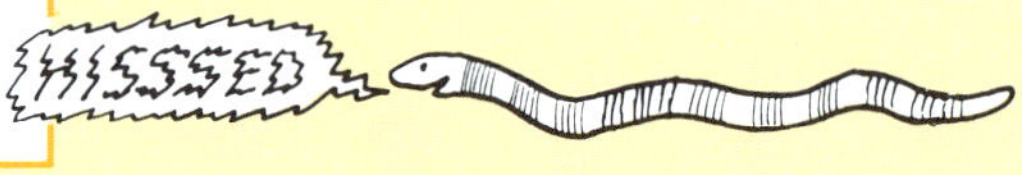

Improving Dialogue

1 Make sure you know how to punctuate and set out dialogue correctly, like this:

Sarah stared hard at Timothy's hand, which seemed to be changing slowly.

"Why is your hand so hairy?" she asked.

"All men's hands are hairy," replied Timothy. "That's normal!"

Sarah frowned and said, "Not that hairy!"

Timothy tried to reply but ...

- Finish this passage.

2 Instead of using the verb 'said' all the time, try some of its synonyms, e.g. replied, asked, cried, moaned. There are many, many more. Look them up in a thesaurus.

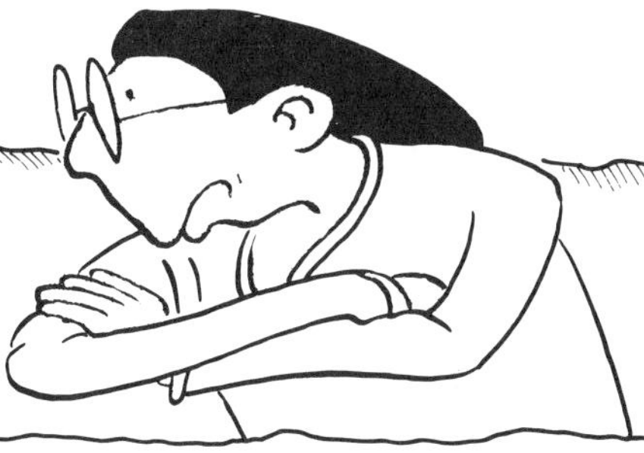

3 "I'm fed up!" *sighed* Sarah.

Add an adverb:

"I'm fed up!" sighed Sarah *moodily*.

4 Add a phrase of description:

"I'm fed up!" sighed Sarah moodily, *throwing herself down on the grass*.

NOW Use these ideas to improve this passage of dialogue.

Sarah slammed her bedroom door and ran downstairs.

"I'm fed up!" she said.

"What's wrong?" said her mum.

"Nothing interesting ever happens to me!" said Sarah.

Suddenly the doorbell rang.

"It's your boyfriend, Timothy," said mum. "He'll cheer you up."

"Hello, Timothy," said Sarah. "You OK?"

"Not bad," he said. "Fancy a moonlight stroll?"

- Finish the story. What happens to Timothy?

Activity

- The activity sheet brings together some of the main techniques in this book and shows how they can be used to improve a piece of writing. The template contains reminders of some of these areas and can be simplified or extended according to the ability of the children you teach.

- The folk tale *Childe Wynd* is typical of many which can be found in children's story books and guide books. They provide a rich source of inspiration for professional writers and are an equally valuable teaching resource.

If children need help, they could be given these suggestions:

Line 1: add an adjective before 'daughter'.
Line 2: add a sentence of description about Margaret and another about the woman.
Line 2: use a conjunction to join the sentences.
Line 3: use a conjunction to join the sentences.
Line 4: add a sentence or two to describe the dragon. Add a few sentences to describe the destruction caused by the dragon.
Line 6: add a sentence to describe Childe Wynd. (Childe is a medieval word meaning 'fighting man/knight'.)
Line 8: add an adjective before 'head'.
Lines 8-9: write the next few lines in dialogue.
Line 10: add an adverb to describe how he kissed the dragon.
Line 12: add an adverb to describe how the dragon burst into flames. Add a sentence to describe Childe Wynd's surprise.
Lines 13-14: write this scene in dialogue.
Line 16: add an adjective before toad.

There are, of course, many other ways of improving this story.

Follow-up

The same technique should be applied to stories written by children and it should become a regular feature of the redrafting process (see page 47). Note that this book has concentrated on improving writing through grammar, but this is only a starting point. Children should also consider style. The best way to do this is through reading and talking about what they have read and also by using key passages from the books they are reading as models. These could be collated as a resource by the teacher or by the children themselves:

- a page of beginnings
- a page of endings
- a page of character descriptions
- a page of place descriptions
- a page of exciting scenes, etc.

- Find other simple folk tales for children to rewrite. These are good for collaborative work and teach children what to look for when they are redrafting their own writing.
- If children get confused by all this terminology, simply say 'add more detail' and they will often be able to improve the story just as effectively. The difference is between a conscious and an unconscious knowledge of what they are doing. The advantage of acquiring a conscious knowledge of the structures of language is that it can help to unravel problems and assist with the handling of more sophisticated structures.

apposite – 'correct', fitting, suitable

Improving Your Writing

The dragon, a huge, fire-breathing beast, was coming.

Improving Your Writing

- Add an adjective or two.
- Add an adverb.
- Join statements with conjunctions to produce more interesting and varied sentences.
- Add a phrase in apposition to improve description.
- Improve dialogue.

noun or noun phrase that renames another right beside it

apposition

two things next to each other

two words or phrases beside each other so that one describes or defines another.

Read this simple folk tale. Work with a partner to make it more interesting using the techniques listed above.

Childe Wynd

Once there was a king in Northumbria. His wife died, leaving him a daughter named Margaret. The King married a woman from the Wild Lands. He did not know she was a witch. The woman was jealous of Margaret's beauty. She changed her into a dragon. The dragon ate flocks of sheep for miles around and burned trees and crops with its breath.

A young knight, Childe Wynd, heard of the dragon. He travelled to Northumbria to destroy it. When he saw it he drew his sword. He was just about to strike off its head when he noticed a tear. He lowered his sword. The dragon told him about the spell that had been cast by the woman of the Wild Lands. It said that Childe Wynd must kiss its lips to break the spell. Childe Wynd did not know what to do. He had heard that dragons were cunning. Was this a trick?

He felt sorry for the dragon so he kissed it. It burst into flames and soon was a heap of ashes. From the ashes rose the Princess Margaret. He took her back to her father who gave Childe Wynd his daughter's hand in marriage and half his kingdom. As for the witch of the Wild Lands, Childe Wynd used her own magic to turn her into a toad. She hopped to a cave beneath the castle where she remains to this day.

Redrafting Checklist - Ideas Bank

Background

The redrafting checklist emphasises the context in which the study of grammar should be placed. It is offered as an example for adaptation rather than for immediate use. When adapting the checklist for the children you teach, the following points should be taken into account:

- The checklist should be closely matched to the age and ability of the children. In practice this may mean that a number of different checklists are in use in the same classroom.
- Younger children and children who are new to self and paired assessment will need much shorter checklists to begin with.
- Include only the categories they are familiar with, e.g. do not refer to adverbs if children have not been introduced to them. This means that the checklists you use will change and develop as the children develop.
- The grammar section in the checklist opposite is the longest, simply because that is the subject of this book. Your own checklist should reflect a better balance.

Follow-up

- Ideally different aspects of teaching should be so closely linked that they reinforce each other. Thus the main points on the Redrafting Checklist are the main teaching points of these grammar activities. In the same way, assessment could be linked into the system by devising an assessment sheet which turns the points on the Redrafting Checklist into 'Can do' statements, e.g.

  - I can write with a specific audience in mind.
  - I can choose words which suit my audience.

  Naturally, this will also need to be linked to the school's assessment system.
- Audience, Purpose and Form. Rather than try to include everything on one sheet, children find it more 'user-friendly' to have shorter, separate sheets. So for example, there might be a Story Checklist including questions about plot, character, description, use of dialogue, etc.
- Similarly, the elements on the checklist opposite could be written on separate sheets, e.g. the grammar could be separate.
- It would be interesting to devise a set of 'CHECKCARDS' which contained just three or four prompts for each area. There could be graded cards for each area, e.g. a very simple card for sentences including the first two points under 'Grammar' opposite, developing to some sophisticated ones which go beyond the points listed opposite.
- The Redrafting Checklist should be seen as an intermediate stage. Children should use it first by themselves, then with a partner. When they become familiar with the process they should be encouraged to manage without it, so that they are more flexible and independent in their approach to redrafting.

CHECKCARD CORRECTNESS

- **Punctuation.** Is the story written in sentences? Does each sentence begin with a capital letter and end with a full stop? Have capital letters been used to begin names of people and places? If speech is used, has it been punctuated correctly? Check it against this pattern.
- **Spelling.** Check the spelling. If in doubt, consult a spelling checklist and a basic word list.
- **Paragraphs.** Is the story set out in paragraphs? Are they used correctly?

Redrafting Checklist

Use this checklist to help you improve your written work. When you have worked through it, find a partner to give you a second opinion. Read your work aloud to him/her, then look at the work together.

AUDIENCE, PURPOSE & FORM

- Who is the audience for the writing?
- Is the choice of words suitable for the audience?
- What is the purpose of the writing?
- How well does it serve its purpose?
- What form is it written in, e.g. story, diary, play, report, article?

GRAMMAR

- Is it written in sentences?
- Does every sentence have a capital letter and a full stop?
- Could any of the sentences be made more descriptive by adding an adjective or adverb?
- Are there too many short sentences? Could some of them be joined by conjunctions?
- Could the description be improved by adding some phrases in apposition?
- Could the dialogue be improved?

LANGUAGE SKILLS

- Check the punctuation, spelling and presentation.

GENERAL

- What did you like best about the piece of writing?
- What do you think could be improved?

NOW IMPROVE YOUR WRITING!

Eight ways to help ...

There are hundreds of ideas in this book to enable you to develop and extend the photocopiable pages. Here are just eight ways to help you make the most of the Ideas Bank series.

1. Photocopy a page, paste on to card and laminate/cover with sticky backed plastic to use with groups. Children can now write on the pages using water-based pens and this can be washed off.

2. Photocopy on to both sides of the paper. Put another useful activity on the back. Develop a simple filing system so others can find relevant sheets and do not duplicate them again.

3. Save the sheets - if the children do not have to cut them up as a part of the activity - and re-use. Label the sets, and keep them safely in files.

4. Make the most of group work. Children working in small groups need one sheet to discuss between them.

5. Put the sheets inside clear plastic wallets. This means the sheets are easily stored in a binder and will last longer. Children's writing can again be wiped away.

6. Use as an ideas page for yourself. Discuss issues with the class and get children to produce artwork and writing.

7. Make an overhead transparency of the page. You and your colleagues can now use the idea time and time again .

8. Ask yourself, "Does every child in this class/group need to deal with/work through this photocopiable sheet?" If not, don't photocopy it!